Contents

Mammals

The animals shown here are all mammals. They are different shapes and sizes because they live different kinds of lives. They come from different parts of the world. All mammals originally lived in the wild, but some are now farm animals or household pets.

▲ This weasel lives in the USA. It creeps along on its short legs. From time to time it stands up to look around.

◄ A gibbon is a kind of **ape**. It lives in the thick forests of south-east Asia. It uses its long arms to swing from tree to tree.

Living Nature

MAMMALS

Chrysalis Children's Books

The publishers wish to thank the following for permission to reproduce copyright material:

Oxford Scientific Films and individual copyright holders on the following pages: Doug Allan 18 bottom; Kathie Atkinson 22; Ron Austing/Photo Researchers Inc 27; Anthony Bannister 10, 16; Eyal Bartov 11 bottom right; Lloyd Beesley/Animals Animals 13 bottom left; Nick Bergkessel/Photo Researchers Inc 19 top; Aldo Brando Leon 17 top left; Carolina Biological Supply Co 13 bottom right; Martyn Colbeck cover, 11 bottom left; Dr J A L Cooke 5 top; Stephen Dalton 25; Tim Davis/Photo Researchers Inc 1; Dr E R Degginger/Animals Animals 11 top; Phil A Dotson/Photo Researchers Inc 4 top; Michael Fogden 15 bottom right; Howard Hall 28/29; Johnny Johnson/Animals Animals 6 top; Hubert Kranemann/Okapia 12 bottom; Dean Lee 7; Leszczynski/Animals Animals 12 top; David Macdonald 15 bottom left; S G Maglione/Photo Researchers Inc 4 bottom; Marty Stouffer Productions/Animals Animals 8/9; Stan Osolinski 3; Richard Packwood 14, 14/15, 23 bottom; Partridge Productions Ltd 24; Robin Redfern 23 top; Hans Reinhard/Okapia 18 top; Philip Sharpe 16/17; Wendy Shattil and Bob Rozinski 26 top; Tony Tilford 17 top right; Steve Turner 5 bottom; Merlin D Tuttle/Photo Researchers Inc 19 bottom; Konrad Wothe 6 bottom; Belinda Wright 26 bottom.

First published in the UK in 2003 by
Chrysalis Children's Books
An imprint of Chrysalis Books Group Plc
The Chrysalis Building, Bramley Road,
London W10 6SP

Paperback edition first published in 2005

Photographs copyright © Oxford Scientific Films and individual copyright holders
Format and illustrations copyright © Chrysalis Books Group Plc

Printed in China

ISBN 1 84138 631 6 (hb)
ISBN 1 84458 384 8 (pb)

British Library Cataloguing in Publication Data CIP data for this book is available from the British Library

Editing: Serpentine Editorial
Senior designer: Frances McKay
Consultant: Andrew Branson

Words in **bold** are in the glossary on page 30.

Title page picture:
A jaguar, one of the largest cats.

Contents page picture:
The gemsbok lives on the grasslands of southern Africa.

◄ Wombats come from Australia. They have small eyes because they live in dark tunnels which they dig under the ground.

Pets such as dogs, cats and hamsters are mammals. So are cows, pigs and sheep. Even people are mammals. All mammals have some things in common that make them different from other animals.

▶ Giraffes are the tallest mammals. They live on the grassy plains of Africa. They use their long necks to reach up and eat the leaves at the top of the trees.

Polar bears have thick fur coats that protect them from the cold and wet conditions of the Arctic.

Fur and hair

Only mammals have hair. It is made of a strong substance called keratin. Fur is thick hair which covers most of the body. Some mammals, such as whales, have little fur.

Others, like the polar bear, have a thick furry coat to keep them warm.

▶ These wolves are fighting. When a wolf is alarmed, the hair on its back stands up to make it look bigger and stronger.

◀ Polar bears live on the frozen Arctic ice. They have a thick layer of fat as well as fur to keep them warm. The underside of their paws is covered with hair to stop them slipping on the ice.

▼ Seals are mammals, too. They swim in cold seawater, using their long, hairy whiskers to feel for food at the bottom of the sea.

Hair protects the skin from heat, cold and wet. It is slightly oily so that water runs off. Each hair is attached to a tiny *muscle* which can make it stand up. When a mammal is cold, its hairs stand up and trap air between them. This keeps the mammal warm.

Did you know?

Hair is not always soft. A rhino's horns are tightly-packed hair, and so are a hedgehog's sharp spikes.

Keeping warm

Mammals do not rely only on their fur to keep them warm. They are warm-blooded animals. This means that their bodies turn some of the food they eat into heat. The blood carries the heat all around the body. So each mammal has its own central heating system. Birds are the only other warm-blooded animals.

▶ Fur, skin and a layer of fat beneath the skin help to keep this hare warm. **Sweat glands** help to cool the animal down when it is hot.

▼ A hungry bobcat chases the snowshoe hare through the snow. Mammals have to eat more food than most animals because they use some of it to make heat.

Did you know?

Musk oxen have the longest hair – almost a metre long. These shaggy animals live in the cold lands near the Arctic.

▶ A tiny piece of a hare's skin magnified many times.

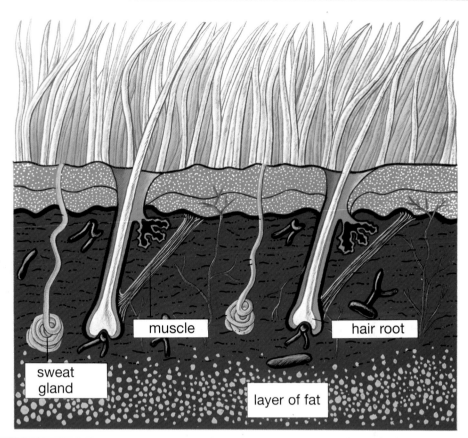

muscle

hair root

sweat gland

layer of fat

Keeping cool

Mammals can get too hot. This may be because they have been running fast, or because they live in a hot place, such as a desert. Mammals have several ways of cooling down. Some have sweat glands (see page 9) which pump salty water on to the skin. As the sweat dries, it cools the skin.

(see page 9)

Did you know?

Camels can travel through the hottest desert. They can go for days without eating or drinking because their hump is a store of fat that is used to provide energy. Camels store heat during the day and cool off at night. They do not sweat or pant and this helps them to stop losing water.

▼ African elephants spray themselves with water to keep cool. Their huge, flappy ears also provide a big surface area to cool the blood.

▼ This small fennec fox lives in the desert. During the hottest part of the day it hides under the ground in a cool **burrow**. At night the fox comes out to hunt.

▲ A coyote is a wild dog. Like all dogs, it pants when it is too hot. It breathes out hot damp air, and takes in cooler air, so its body cools down from the inside.

▲ This warthog has rolled in a cool, muddy pool. As the mud dries, its skin is cooled.

Making milk

A mammal mother does not have to find food for her young. She feeds her newborn babies with her own supply of milk.

▲ Two black bear cubs suck milk from their mother's teats. Milk is made in the **mammary glands** and contains all the food the cubs need. All mammals have mammary glands, sometimes called breasts or udders.

▶ Humans are mammals, too. This baby will feed only on its mother's milk until it is four months old. Then it will start to eat solid food as well.

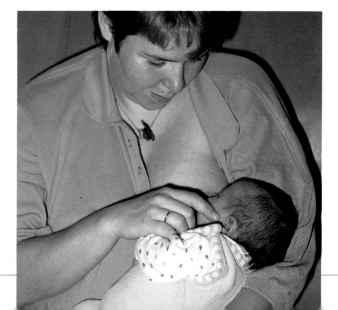

▼ A baby duck-billed platypus hatches from its egg.

Kangaroos, koalas and wombats are all marsupials. The babies are born before they are fully formed, and crawl through their mother's fur into her pouch. They stay there, drinking her milk, while they grow.

▲ The duck-billed platypus lays eggs instead of giving birth to babies. The eggs hatch about ten days after they are laid, but the babies are still very small.

▼ Opossums are marsupials. Newborn opossums are tiny, naked and blind. They crawl into their mother's pouch and drink her milk.

◄ As they grow bigger the baby possums leave their mother's pouch.

Growing up

All young mammals have to be looked after by their parents. Some mammals make a **den** where the young can hide until they are able to walk and look after themselves. Other young mammals can walk soon after they are born.

▼This hunting dog pup is big enough to leave the den, but its mother still watches over it.

▲ Newborn wildebeest have long, wobbly legs. They can follow their mothers almost at once.

Mammals are cleverer than other animals. Most animals act from **instinct**, but mammals can think and learn. They learn how to hunt and survive by copying the adults. Human children take nearly 20 years to learn to be adults.

◀ Meerkats live in large groups. This adult meerkat is looking after all the young while the other adults hunt.

▼ A baby sloth clings to its mother's fur as she carries it slowly through the trees.

Walking and running

Most mammals move about on four legs. When they walk they move only one leg at a time, but when they run, all four legs can be in the air at the same time.

Many mammals walk on tiptoe and some have hoofs to protect their toes.

◄ This African antelope grips the steep rock with its hoofs. Hoofs, claws and nails are made of keratin, like hair (see page 7).

▲ The huge capybara comes from South America. It walks on its toes but puts its whole foot down when it wants to rest. What looks like a knee is really an ankle.

▼ A cheetah speeds through the grass on its long legs. Like many mammals, it has pads behind its claws to help it grip the ground.

▲ The tiny pygmy shrew walks on the soles of its feet. It scratches for insects with its long toes.

Swimming and flying

Some mammals live in the sea. Seals, walruses, whales and dolphins have long, slim bodies like fish. They use their flippers to push themselves through the water. Unlike fish, sea mammals cannot breathe in water. They come to the surface to gulp in air.

▲ A kangaroo can jump six metres. It uses the large muscles on its back legs to jump.

◄ Sea mammals are fast swimmers. This leopard seal has just caught a young penguin.

Many mammals are good swimmers, but bats are the only mammals that can fly. Their wings are made of skin stretched between their long, thin fingers. Bats are hard to see because they only fly in the dark.

▲ The flying squirrel cannot really fly. It has large flaps of skin between its front and back legs which it stretches out like a wing. The squirrel can jump from high branches and glide from tree to tree. It uses its tail to steer.

▶ Bats are the only mammals that can really fly. This bat is about to catch an insect.

Did you know?

The sperm whale can hold its breath for up to 1.5 hours as it dives down over 1000 metres under the sea.

Teeth and jaws

incisor

You can tell what kind of food a mammal eats by its teeth. Meat-eaters have four large, sharp canine teeth towards the front of their mouths which they use to grasp their **prey**. Plant-eaters have flat back teeth for chewing plants.

▲ Cats have many pointed teeth at the back of their mouths for cutting up meat. Their jaws move up and down.

pointed teeth   canine

◄ Deer have large, flat back teeth for grinding down plants. Their jaws move from side to side. The front of their mouths have bottom teeth only.

incisors

back (cheek) teeth

All mammals have sharp incisor teeth at the front of their mouths. Incisors are good for scraping meat off bones or cutting plants.

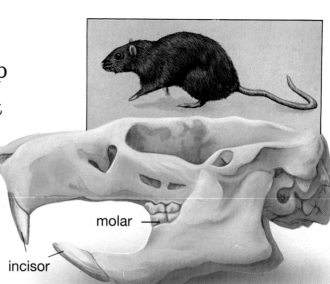

molar

incisor

Did you know?

Elephant and walrus tusks are two huge teeth. The elephant uses its tusks to dig for water and roots. Walruses lever themselves on to ice floes with their tusks and use them to scrape shellfish from the seabed.

▲ Rats have long, sharp teeth at the front of their mouths for gnawing through nuts and other hard foods.

▶ Apes eat both meat and plants. Some of their teeth are sharp, others are flat. Their jaws move up and down and from side to side.

incisor

canine

molar

▲A spiny anteater has a long nose and a very long, sticky tongue. It uses them to find and catch ants and other insects.

Smelling

Smells are very important to most mammals. They use their noses to sniff out food. Most mammals make their own special smell or scent. Some mammals, such as cats and mice, follow their noses to find a **mate**.

◀ Each mammal smells different. Rats and other mammals use their sense of smell to recognize each other. Newborn mammals soon learn their mother's smell so that they can find her even if they cannot see.

▼ Some mammals use smell to mark out their **territory**. Lions and dogs, such as wolves, mark the edges of their territory with **urine**. Then other mammals know to keep away.

Hearing

▶ A mammal's ears are different from those of other animals. The **eardrum** is inside the ear and three small bones pass sound on to the brain. Reptiles, birds and frogs have just one bone.

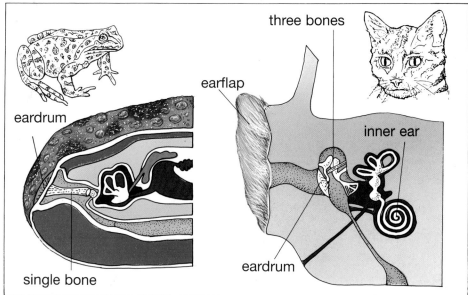

three bones

earflap

inner ear

eardrum

eardrum

single bone

Most mammals rely on hearing as well as smell and sight to warn them of danger. They are the only animals that have earflaps on the outside of their heads to collect the sound. Sound passes down the ear channel to the eardrum.

◀ This marsh deer lives in Brazil. It is always listening for danger. Its large ears turn to pick up the slightest sound.

▶ This diagram shows how the sound from a bat bounces off an insect to make an echo.

Bats use sound to find their way in the dark. They make very high-pitched clicks or squeaks. When the sounds hit an object they bounce back. A bat can tell where an object is by listening for these echoes.

◀ Bats use their ears to find out where their prey is in the dark. They listen for echoes bouncing off it.

Seeing

Animals that are hunted usually have eyes in the sides of their heads. They watch out for danger all around them.

▲ A rabbit has eyes in the sides of its head. It can see in front and on both sides at the same time.

▶ A tiger's eyes are in the front of its head. The tiger **focuses** on what is in front of it.

Meat-eaters have their eyes in the front of their heads. This helps them to judge distance exactly so that they know how far to pounce to catch their prey.

◄ Tarsiers have big eyes to help them see at night.

World of mammals

There are about 4000 different kinds of mammal. They live in most parts of the world, in deserts, jungles, oceans and even in the Arctic.

▶ Dolphins are mammals, even though they spend all their lives at sea. They come to the surface to breathe and their young are born under water.

All mammals, even those that live in the sea, have hair and feed their young with their milk.

No other animals can do this. Mammals are also able to think more than other animals. Humans are the cleverest animals of all.

Did you know?

Dolphins are cleverer than most mammals. They 'talk' to each other using various squeaks and calls. Dolphins have also rescued drowning swimmers by nudging them to the surface of the water.

Glossary

Apes Monkey-like animals that are like human beings. They have no tail and walk for much of the time on two legs.

Burrow An underground home which an animal digs for itself and its family. It can be just a hole, or may be made up of several tunnels and chambers.

Den A wild animal's home. It may be any sheltered space, such as a cave or a gap among the roots of a tree. Female polar bears make dens in the snow in which they give birth to their young.

Eardrum A membrane, like thin skin, across the ear canal. Sound waves make the eardrum vibrate or move up and down.

Focus To see a clear picture. When an animal has two eyes in the front of its head, each eye sees an object at a slightly different angle. The brain makes these two pictures into one. This gives a 3D effect which allows the animal to judge distance.

Instinct Knowing what to do without thinking. Animals find a mate and defend themselves by instinct.

Mammary glands A special part of a female mammal's body which produces milk.

Mate One of a pair of animals – one male, one female – who together produce young.

Muscle Meaty substance inside the body which makes the bones and other parts of the body move.

Prey An animal that is hunted for food by another animal.

Sweat glands Tiny structures in the skin which produce a salty liquid.

Territory An area of ground in which an animal hunts. Many animals mark their territory with their own scent.

Urine Waste water and poisons which the body expels through the kidneys and bladder.

Key facts

Largest mammal The blue whale is the largest mammal and also the largest animal that has ever lived. It grows to 30 metres long – as long as three buses parked end to end.

Heaviest mammal This is the blue whale, too. It weighs about 3 tonnes when it is born and up to 190 tonnes when it is fully grown – as heavy as 2000 people, or 52 buses.

Heaviest land mammal An African elephant can weigh up to 7 tonnes – heavier than 80 people.

Tallest mammal Giraffes can reach 5.5 metres high. Three people would have to stand on each other's shoulders to be able to stroke a giraffe's head.

Smallest mammal The tiny hog-nosed bat from Thailand weighs only 2 grams and is no bigger than a bumblebee.

Fastest mammal Cheetahs can sprint at 112 kilometres per hour, as fast as a car on a motorway.

Slowest mammal Sloths hang upside down on the branches of trees in the South American rainforest. They hardly move at all, but when they do they move very slowly.

Longest jumper Red kangaroos can jump more than 12 metres in one bound, further than an Olympic athlete and as far as three cars parked end to end.

Largest bat When Malay fruit bats stretch out their wings they measure about 1.5 metres from wing tip to wing tip. This is as big as an eagle.

Biggest burrows Prairie dogs dig underground burrows which connect with each other, like a vast underground town. Most prairie dogs now live mainly in nature reserves.

Gentlest giants Gorillas are the largest apes and grow nearly 2 metres tall. They are very strong but they are not fierce. They eat leaves, fruit, vegetables and twigs.

Index